Additional Praise for

ENGINE

EMPIRE

"Cathy Park Hong is a seer of visions. *Engine Empire* is a brainy, glinting triptych about what powers 'progress,' what its human costs are, and where it might be taking our species. Novelistic, meditative, offbeat, and soulful, Hong's poetry is many fathoms deep." —David Mitchell

"This deeply original work dramatically engages the current state of the condition we call America as it hurtles toward some unspeakable future. The speaker wants to rebuild history. It keeps breaking. There is no story, no verse form, no vessel of voice that holds. And yet each fragment is unbroken, perfect, and perfectly renders the icily lit unfixability of it all. One thinks of Berryman, of Tom Sawyer and Jim, of Plenty Coups, last great chief of the Crow, all the while hearing a country western tune in an overturned car where this boomtown goes bust. But it is a necessary bust. Hong's brilliant soul knows it and is ready for the hard ride toward change." —Jorie Graham

"Cathy Park Hong widens the planet's ambit with her polyphonous poems, drawing more dimension from a single vowel than most can coax from an entire alphabet. Out of bastard tongues and artful boomtown constructions, Hong fashions a history so peculiar and precise as to transcend simile, to stand as a bona-fide prophetic vision. *Engine Empire* represents that rarest triumph of the imagination: poetry whose astral body dwells both here and in the subsequent world." —D. A. Powell

"Hong's lexical inventiveness is an absolute joy, a countercurrent to the bleak past present and future she describes. *Engine Empire* presents a lineup of tragicomic characters, including a Chinese forger of Rembrandts named Rembrandt and a boy named 'Orright' by his father, an avid Anglophile. The futurist 'World Cloud' section features chilling 'smart snow' that reads your mind and a glacier invading a stadium. This is a riveting rabbit hole of a book."   —Matthea Harvey

ENGINE EMPIRE

Cathy Park Hong

W. W. NORTON & COMPANY

NEW YORK · LONDON

For information about permission to reproduce selections from this book,
write to Permissions, W. W. Norton & Company, Inc.,
500 Fifth Avenue, New York, NY 10110

For information about special discounts for bulk purchases, please contact
W. W. Norton Special Sales at specialsales@wwnorton.com or 800-233-4830

Manufacturing by Sterling Pierce
Book design by JAMdesign
Production manager: Julia Druskin

Library of Congress Cataloging-in-Publication Data

Hong, Cathy Park.
Engine empire / Cathy Park Hong. — 1st ed.
p. cm.
Poems.
ISBN 978-0-393-08284-5
I. Title.
PS3608.O494438E54 2012
811'.6—dc23
2012000596

ISBN 978-0-393-34648-0 pbk.

W. W. Norton & Company, Inc.
500 Fifth Avenue, New York, N.Y. 10110
www.wwnorton.com

W. W. Norton & Company Ltd.
15 Carlisle Street, London W1D 3BS
5 6 7 8 9 0

For Mores

Contents

Acknowledgments

Grateful acknowledgment is made to *A Public Space, The Paris Review, Lana Turner, Poetry, Conjunctions, Web Conjunctions, Boston Review, Octopus, McSweeney's, Triple Canopy, Parnassus, Witness, Fence, American Poetry Review, Lo-Ball,* and *Harvard Review* where some of these poems first appeared.

Thank you to the following residencies for giving me time: The Macdowell Colony, Yaddo, Bellagio Center, and Fundacion Valparaiso.

Thank you to my editor, Jill Bialosky, for her support.

My gratitude to family and friends who have helped engine this book along: Sung Dal Hong, Haesook Hong, Nancy Hong, Ghita Schwarz, Evie Shockley, Jonathan Thirkield, Meghan O'Rourke, Martha Collins, Adam Schecter, Joe Winter, Gary Shteyngart, Jen Liu, Thomas Sayers Ellis, and Doug Choi.

He heard the snow falling faintly through the universe
and faintly falling, like the descent of their last end,
upon all the living and the dead.

—James Joyce

ENGINE
EMPIRE

BALLAD
OF OUR JIM

Fort Ballads

Ballad of the Range

The whole country is in a duel and we want no part of it.
They see us ride, they say
:all you men going the wrong di-rection.
:We're getting to California. We ain't got time to enlist.

If some forts ready to be sawed to colt towns,
others are abandoned since ricket-limbed Southies
couldn't let their grudges aside and mauled
each other to blood strops.

All around us forts lie built and unbuilt, half-
walled towns as men yoke themselves to state,
but we brothers are heading through fields of blue rye and plains
scullground to silt sand,

afar, the boomtowns of precious ore.

Ballad of Fort Mann

Come to a fort of ragged cedar posts,
rigged together by rodent sinews of prairie dogs.
We holler and little boys peek from above,
their faces seared by blast wind.

:Who you be? What you want? They shout thinly.

Boys in rags and twine suspenders hold Winchesters
much too big for them. They aim at us.
:Where all yer pops?
:They at war!

We lost a brother, axed in the head by a rancid trapper,
so we pluck one boy from the litter,
lure him out with hen fruit and fresh violet marrow.
We pounce him. Christen him Jim.

But our adapted boy's head done turned.
All he does is sing, his throat a tender lode of tern flutes
disturbing our herd, singing of malaria,
his murderous, lime-corroded Ma.

Ballad of Heel Squatter Canyon

The land shocks up to a clay
escarpment up to towers of Cretaceous cliffs
burrowed with a thousand snake holes
like an Aztec civilization forgotten.

Against this heathen monument, we make camp.

At night, a grand illumination:
the prairie grass licking up in a widening, spiraling fire.
A herd of antelope spring out
from that conflagration so far from us

they're fleas leaping from pelt
yet Our Jim shoots one easy as varmint
and we fast reckon this queer
piper can tame this fickle, harrowed land.

Ballad of Infanticide

Near starved, we find a fort of teetotalers
who begrudge us their succor.

While we eat up all their salt pork,
Our Jim sings for them in his strange high voice
of an Injun killing ranger who hitches up
with his Comanche guide.

She bears him a strapping son and is ramped
with another, when the ranger hives off
with a fair-haired sheriff's daughter.
He then banishes his squaw and his sons
like they're prairie beeves.

But she won't go quietly:
she poisons his new wife with a malarial dress,
and that ain't the worst of her sins, that tar-eyed witch
strangles her own newborn,
and the other son flees—

The ladies cry: enough of this devil song.
Then it done occurs to us, looking at his dusky skin—

Our Jim's a two-bit half-breed.

Mob Ballad

A beet-red adobe acropolis with a guano-
whitened belfry. Missing is its function, the great bell,
so it frames only grayish light,
a harping muteness.

But then we hear the gropping cries.

A horsehair tightrope tied from one barrack to another,
and the crowd jeers and rails
til a rouge-doused banker in a stovepipe hat
is pushed from the balcony, trembling against the ledge.

:Walk it you rotten cheat.

they shoot and he flinches, dances without meaning,
they fire again til he fumbles one foot on the rope
and before he makes his second, he falls,
too fast for us to even see his suspended froggish body

the thud, his silence.
They ain't one bit sated, so full
their pent.

Ballad of Tombstone Omaha

Day's gone immortal.

The bleached ruin of light lasts and lasts, no night
to repair our minds, no white clip moon to give us rest,
Only pitiless noon where our sleep-starved consciousness
patters faintly behind our squinted eyelids.

Then, sod homes, no bigger than raised graves and inside,
none dwelled, only nail keg and soap box for chairs.
We sacked the sod home down,
drank dram beer.

As we pulled the last of the spuds,
Phantom harridans raged from these mounds to chase us down,
earth crusted to their salt skin as if God didn't finish
his making and we shot, shot, shot

and nothing but plovers rose into the air.

Ballad of Rites Inside a Rookery of Avarice

This is the last barricaded fort we pass.
Men of faith and the whores they cured have taken reign,
using brandy cask-rigged pulpits
to mete out their punition.

Whores have a fandango to celebrate one man
hung and dry lightning splits

while preachers swaddle the other thief
like an Indian babe in winter, and they carouse
while he measles sweat. One bastard child
whips him fast on the ear.

A preacher hitches Our Jim to a shaking post
and his leppy body trembles to a million ticks,
a foreboding of what's to come.
:He's in you. He's in you now!

Our Jim cries from such an invasion.
:No one never in me. No one.

Ballad of the Occasional Indian Disturbance

Our Jim kills our first, a Miwok, who done tried to sneak
off with our mules. For days, we drug his gutted body, tailed
by a lariat of vultures who peck him raw,
a procession of wild, piss-eyed lobos.

His sister rears the parade.

When we break for camp, she alights on us like a woolen moth,
begs us for his body so she can mourn him.
We stomp at her, unload our pistols near her, still she begs
and so we take her hard.

Later, she keens a wretched song til one
of us brothers, tired of her yammerings,
unhooks the gnawed-on body
from the wagon.

Our Jim's gone husk.
He warns us of our weakness.

Ballad Beyond the Forts

We stop speaking. Our lips curl back so we're just teeth.
Our Jim sings as if all his body's reed.
No thought flickers behind his linseed eyes.
Soon we're the same,

A small parasite bore into our bellies
and memories slide out like gut. We kill
the few pickings of buffalo, butchering their huge
roddled heads, their liver tongues.

Blood bursts from Earth's throat
in a mighty tornado and speckles itself across
the soil, hardening to ruby poppies.
A mighty empire arises.

Ballad of Grace

But the mighty empire is a false pond
in this eternal light where night never descends,
where we pass old travelers forever dying, their lamb-milk eyes
astonished by years passing as one long noon.

It is here we call Our Jim to drain
them of the last dregs of their consciousness
he shoots them easy as horses and
we move on, passing

a legendary mining town drained of its ore
yet still, still the isolated men settle to dig
and dig, furrowing wilder
into the earth.
We see the empire rising.

Ballad in O

O Boomtown's got lots of sordor:
odd horrors of throwdowns,
bold cowboys lock horns,
forlorn hobos plot to rob

pots of gold, loco mobs
drool for blood, howl or hoot
for cottonwood blooms, throng
to hood crooks to strong wood posts.

So don't confront hotbloods,
don't show off, go to blows or rows,
don't sob for gold lost to trollops,
don't drown sorrows on shots of grog.

Work morn to moon.
Know how to comb bottom pools,
spot dots of gold to spoon pots of gold.
Vow to do good.

Abecedarian Western

Ate stew, shot a man,
Bandy body spraddled, so full of lead
Cabrón can't even walk uphill
Derringer spit out of bullets
Empty as a gutted steer
Found a soiled dove,
Got me some cash roll for a night.
Hacienda next dawn,
Indian scalps round my neck.
Jacal shack full of hunched men
Kicked that hut down,
Limped them with shots,
Morning to scalp them,
Noontime, sang.
Offal yarned in one satchel saddle
Prairie oyster in the other,
Quit the flats, into town
Raised on prunes and proverbs
Scorched a church,
Threw down a priest hiding
Under mesquite shrub and blatting woolies,
Vaquero packs me with iron,
Wastes me easy as if
X marked my vest plain as
Yucca country.
Zanjero digs a ditch.

Ballad in A

A Kansan plays cards, calls marshal
a crawdad, that barb lands that rascal a slap;
that Kansan jackass scats,
camps back at caballada ranch.

Hangs kack, ax, and camp hat.
Kansan's nag mad and rants can't bask,
can't bacchanal and garland a lass,
can't at last brag can crack Law's balls,

Kansan's cantata rang at that ramada ranch,
Mañana, Kansan snarls, I'll have an armada
and thwart Law's brawn,
slam Law a damn mass warpath.

Marshal's a marksman, maps Kansan's track,
calm as a shaman, sharp as a hawk,
says: that dastard Kansan's had
and gnaws fatback.

At dawn, marshal stalks that ranch,
packs a gat and blasts Kansan's ass
and Kansan gasps, blasts back.
A flag flaps half-staff.

Man that Scat

I'm a natty crossdressing
wrastler in possum
chaps, my boots can smash
any clapboard slat,

I'm a crass buscadero, wild-
eyed thumber, hired killer,
leather slapping keener,
a no kin outlaw,

I foe alone in these one
horse boombusted towns
take my time blasting
addled sherriffs.

Sing my glotten track,
my Sierran Pastern,
I will loot in spades
these tarnishing yarns.

I cant my rambling
jabber like a carnage
starved lobo.
My yipping's hazard.

Bowietown Ballads

Ballad of Arrival with Hatajo of Mules

We shuck our boots near an alkali pond
where no fish breathes its poison, only white alien worms
float like dander from a sunken
corpse turned angel.

We howl our inborn call:

Jim! Pitch them raw hide tents,
tie yonder tarrope to strip wood,
we'll yamp this land and build upon it.

Our clamguns chink down the hardened
earth, our pickaxes chip bone,
only bone, no glittering dust,
we sulk into our loam.

Ballad of Other Folk

They keep on coming, cowpokes and canvas-wagoned
Easterners trailing through graveyards
of footsore beeves to this gant
sapling town

as if this salt-encrusted pond
washed them up out of foam:
Mexicans and deacon-sized Chinamen
who find what we cain't find.

One Chinaman gets knifed fer being what he is.
Another strikes it rich and apes us
wearing silver spurs and possum chaps,
dancing a spry little jig.

What is the clear word?
Shred the other folk.

Ballad of the Rube Parade with Their Quiver of Spades

Nights we gamble with henchmen French
who warn us they used to hack rebels
when it was hellfire revolution in their land.
Still they lust for human game.

Our Jim starts singing his infernal ballad—
:Shut yer trap Jim.

He watches silent as our game
ratchets to pistolfire brawl.
Goddamnfilthy French gores us so ropes
of blood gout from our brother's gullet

We scream: Do it boy! Shoot!
He aims cold, slays them all,
exciting us no end.
He says: I'm done finishing your games.

Ballad of Burial Rites and the Effigy of Vengeance

The last Chief lived a bitter century, born
when buzzard-headed gods roamed these tawny foothills,
and now, his kin leads his carrion cradled
in a hoodlum wagon;

They done lampblacked their faces,
and ask for scrap wood
so they can burn his body in a glittering pyre.

Banged up on bug juice, we laugh at their gibber,
until one of our brothers scatters the parade,
tips the wagon, and the Chief slumps out
in a heap of bones.

Next morning, we find our brother hung
like a sheet of meat. Neckbone snapped,
jaw shrunk in: they yanked out
all his teeth.

Ballad of a Mercy Killing

Yuccas gnarl out with red spider buds.
Once men unspared, praying to be unstitched
from earth, crying: let us free to roam,
wade into shadow so the flayed

red threads of our soul can cool to will
and we can spread our spores,
and if we fail, He will smite us.

Our brother drowns of conscious.
He spills onto the street, cracking his head
with a clay jug, then rakes
his blooded face with the anguish

of a burning dog. My Jim
comes, dear boy, do it,
no don't and shoots him to a batter
of brain and dust.

Ballad of Unbidding

Our Jim's gone deadmouthed, won't respond
to our bit, his head's a petrified den tree—
and some ursine beast from tarnation
is holed up inside it.

For nothing, he blows out a retired lawman,
gunfanning buck nun sheriffs who ramble
in from dried out towns to sniff out
fortune.

Ghosts weed out their bodies,
whispering into sun's paling twilight,
glazing into clouds and glass needled
rain shatters the dusted tundra,

He slays them before they breed to corps.
Still they come, an eternal train of settlers,
chapels of ruby coppered hills flattened
by the agate ants of strangers.

Ballad of a Showdown

And then he sarved up a high grass constable,
an old techy ranger hailed for bringing order to the land.
And the Law finally put a mighty
bounty on his head.

All night, a showdown of lungs aired,
flint scrabble of hooves, pop of pistolfire
All night, the geezer hollered, panted,
screaming: show yer face!

Could have predicted the end,
windstorm feasting on the old man's belly fiddle,
boy's whorled eyes an aqueduct of boiled black oil
shambling off to sleep for Our Jim's still a boy
no matter what they—

When we heard about the reward,
we last two brothers decided to do him in.

The Testimonial of the Last Brother

Why we fools hatched to drug and drain
him in his sleep.

But he sang in his dreams, so raw
he sucked us inside his fevered innards:
a cloudburst of a horse rising to a stolen remuda
as if all Mexico was raided: stallions, peg ponies, hogbacks—
Git out he cried yet we were boiled
inside him where

we saw a cross-dressing squaw in chaps,
charging that mutant, mural herd through Bowietown,
trampling down our tallowed kip tents, knocking
down engine cars packed with forfeit
ore—*Git out.*

We tumbled out his dream.
His ears so keen he woke once he heard us
cock our pistol he leapt at us, wrestling our gun away.

It was my brother Campbell who fell to his knees
and blubbered: Why Jim we adopted—
Jim shot him so hard that bullet ripped through
his head and skimmed my jaw.

Then I shut my eyes real tight.

Don't know how long I waited before I reckoned,
he was gone.

Ballad in I

Sing in this blinking twilight,
in this mining district filling with wild
Irish striking it rich, spinning
Christ, swigging spirits, rigging spits,

picking fights, swinging fists,
slitting twitching skin in livid fits,
crippling limbs, spitting kinnikinnick,
filling trim tins with hissing piss.

His mind's still spiting, knifing with skill,
his victimizing intrinsic within his mind,
grinding within his skin,
Jim sings: I'm tiring, I'm tiring.

His grim instinct wilting.
Dispiriting Jim, climbing hill's hilt,
drifting Jim, sighing in this lilting,
sinking light.

The Song of Katydids

He rides into a shadowed plain,
where a storm of grasshoppers
hoving wings to wind,
blacks the sky thick as larrup.

These pests drop to earth,
clumping on every growth,
sucking sweat from all tooled handles,
a rogue insectile rug is the land.

Then he sees her with a nibbling
chain of grasshoppers clipping away
tendril strands of her hair
as she bats the bug-furred corn.

He stops, done in and gasps
with the first feelings of want.
He struggles to her, blinded by insects,
and shouts with his little Spanish: *¡Te Quiero!*

Even in that mandible storm, her ma
knows him as the killer outlaw
and snatches her daughter away.
She spits so luxuriously on the ground,

she drowns a hopper,
and pulls her child back into their sod-
battened home, so he is alone
in the roar of all nibbling,

which clings, stains and gnaws
his leather raiment to bitten lace.
He clamps his hands to his ears
from all the bedlamite mouths rising

and just as suddenly, the insects
spur their wings and fly farther off,
leaving Jim be, to go
in the denuded earth.

SHANGDU, MY ARTFUL BOOMTOWN!

Year of the Pig

8.I

Brother, we were enthralled by massif dead pigs floating
downriver   we hauled butchered   feasted
then squalled for it was rotted meat.
Sickest of bipeds we were but monks prayed for us,
cured us of our rankled bodies.
Also, the new observatory's been ransacked for its myths,
the telescope shattered to a million bifocals,
the furrier uses 'em now to sew tiny rabbit mitts
w' pearlseed beads for babes
of the landlord foe.

10.I

We found out who it was: during hellswelt summer, his pigs
turned spotted and keeled over all at once
the earth was already cramped w' the buried,
so his limp daughter and he threw the loadsome rotted crits
into the river
and the river slewed them down to us.

Brother, we tried him and decided he was guilty.

II.I

Years turning worsome since you've left,
allow me to give you my rundown:

year of the rat: I0 yields of sorghum.
year of the dragon: I0 yields of sorghum.
year of the dog: I yield of sorghum.

year of the monkey: a drought. A lowland huckster arose
and told us our idle highland's perfect for his *eye to all the stars,*
an observatory that will attract pilgrims from afar.
We will all make a goodly profit. Like fools, we sell.

year of the snake: a fraud telescope that shewed
not the promised swirling world of distant suns.
We line to look and see nothing but the flat hazen sky
we always see when we strike our loam.

2.9

I am covetous of you and curse our birth order,
I long for lightspeed Shangdu.
Brother, imagine me.

I tilled and tilled our narrow plot from daybreak to cinder dusk.
When you write about the 400 string lights,
you and your new wife hurting w' laughter
on a duck-shaped boat

do you know your laughter carries isself to our lornsome hills
and flushes my ears when I feed
Ma her broth?

Can I join you, Brother? Do you have room for me?

4.5

Ma has passed   the village gathered and wailed w' trumpet lungs,
while I daydreamed of leaving these parched shriven hills,
traveling far into the mirror cast of Shangdu's
chandeliering lights,

Then that melon-bellied landlord, a genius
for making tithes, skulked by and tithed me, tithed the grievers,
who quickly scrambled to escape the tithe,

tithed our ma for the burial.
Even the dead don't escape the tithe.

5.5

Year of the pig: at last the rain has come
for days it slews and grows the trefoiled, mossclung trees,
and teastained dotted moths.

I've tilled the bit of unsold land.
I've tilled and tilled and done what I've been told.
Brother, I've tilled and tilled and always done,
I've always done what I've been told.

Brother, why have you not written?
Brother, can I join you?

Aubade

I long for harmine morning to lift me
from my hisshurled life but my
hellwhelmed county of harsh scruffed
crops is marooned, my plow a beached
whale's browbone on morose miles of moor.
Heft heft. I cry to my ox
but no hint of green wort. Just midges
to torment my ox. You intone
forego lament, willingly forfeit the ai-ai.
so I slaughter my ox. So hi-hi!
I am ready in my plaidwhelmed
puffpuff golf hat. Ready to be
whelmed by a petstore cacophony
of crickets shirruping in their cage balls,
juddering slam of hammering jack,
humming sussurations of catamarans,
aerosol striations of welder's firecrack,
then a caracas of fist cracks
after workers slurp off their goggled specs
to a bassooning fog horn hooning
so spooning lovers know when to return
to their dawn shift, tuning cymbals
for toy baboons who clap clap,
Hail the Industrial Age, hail!

Market Forces Are Brighter Than the Sun

My Aleph, My Grand Dame, My Turks
frozen in time! Haroon, Kadoori, Sassoon
with your bolts of canary silk sheared
and sold down Shangdu's river alongside
a wedding of gamblers betting in a vintage sampan.
Barges of creaky banquet halls,
spit out your prawn tail in this ramekin! Shots
of Crown Royal for all! Dear natty vessel
of chemical dye, dear floating factory
of cleaning supplies, let me buy
you out, my wire hanger is mannered
like the virgin neck of a Parmigianino nude,
my lint roller can defur a Pomeranian dog.
Shangdu, my artful boomtown,
I will smudge out your horizon line with my
thumb, I will stuff you cheek to jowl
and pipette you with petrol,
chasing out urchins nibbling on beetle kebabs!
Foreigners, do nip from that Blue Label
in our train which is faster than the Shinkansen,
powered by our merry laughs:
Ho Ho Ho! Ha Ha Ha! Ho Ho Ho!
Xiao, bring me my napkin,
my thumb is smudged with the horizon.

Adventures in Shangdu

Of Lucky Highrise Apartment 88

The contractors were in a hurry to catch up with the rest of the world
so they rushed off before they finished building Highrise 88. So here
is my apartment without its last wall, gaping out to a panoramic view
of Shangdu's river. Across the river, all the white-tiled factories hum
anxiously. This hum of 2,000 factories can inspire or drive you mad.
Yesterday, a drunk man and a suicide used 88's unencumbered views
to fall to their deaths and now there are ads for new roommates. I
am one of the few women who live alone in this building. My last
roommate married as quickly as she moved in with me. I see her in
the neighborhood, pregnant and gloating, with men who fetch her
footstools.

Of Lucky Highrise Apartment 88's Courtyard or Epithalamion

When a gale of wind lifts the guile of newsprint and a feast of quails
stanches the stench of our units, a crowd will yearn and follow. Once,
they followed the smell and then they saw the age difference between
the marrying couple: an old haggard widow and a young fresh-
scrubbed boy of 20. She was stoop-shouldered in carnation red and he
was in crisped blue suit. When the couple kissed, the mob made their
presence known and heckled their ritual wedlock. Not rice they threw,
but spit. Yet still, they watched while cackling, wistful as the fried
prawn vendor who turned his surveillance camera toward the rising
and setting sun.

Of the Millennial Promenade Along the River

Vendors line the promenade to serve passersby—they sell pinwheels, pancakes and roast meats of all kinds, even sticks of prickly little seahorses. One female vendor keeps peeled apples under her armpit until they are saturated with her scent and then she sells them so customers can luxuriate in both the scent of fruit and her ripeness. Along the promenade, the rabble is enraptured by the new tower across the river but the vendors grumble of slow business. Officials installed cameras behind the vendor's umbrella fringes to catch conspirators. Today, there is no drama so the vendors gossip.

It is true that the fried prawn vendor tilted his surveillance camera so it caught nothing but the sun. Officials executed him after they watched the useless footage of a sun bobbing up and down for 100 days. Why did he do such a stupid thing? He was a saboteur! said one. We should all destroy the cameras. Everyone knows about them and it takes away business! Said a third, It was for personal reasons. He was stupid in love and his lover walked out on him for—and the vendors stopped short for the cameras were recording.

Of the Old Colonial Dutch Quarters

When I imagine this city, it is not the city that I want but the city that I fear. But I too have an obsession. He is one of the painters who works in the Rembrandt factory. He paints 5 Rembrandt self-portrait paintings a day which I hear are sold to rich town houses and hotels in a place called Florida. He is renowned as the fastest painter in Shangdu and he has completed 10,000 Rembrandt self-portraits. In the mornings, I walk past him when he is on his smoke break. Today, I catch him sniffing his hand.

Of the Street of Xiaos

There they are, squatting all in row. We call them stick-stick soldiers. Unmarried migrant men who wander in from the rural provinces. If a scooter were to crash into a poultry truck, they would be the first to rush and gawk at the accident. If a foreigner were to sit at a café, they would gather around the foreigner and gape until the foreigner left the café from self-consciousness. While others are active verbs who *do,do,do*, Xiaos are the true helping verbs. Sometimes, they sponge white over graffiti, pave potholed roads, or scrub the sauna's drained tubs until there is enough dirt and dander in their pails to make another Xiao. Here, another foreigner arrives and sits outside and the Xiaos crowd around to stare. When the foreigner speaks the language, they are delighted. They ask, Are you Jewish? When he says no, they are disappointed and walk away.

Of the New Star Sauna at Merchant Road

An anchorman met his new assistants for lunch and asked if they knew how famous he was. As if on cue, two people came and shook his hand. A waitress poured him his English tea and he told her to wait by his tea until it was fully steeped. She stood quietly and then he laughed and told her it was just a test. Later that day, she visited the newly built sauna. Everywhere around her, people exfoliated themselves with coarse pads, shedding delicate shades of skin to forget their harrowing day. She left the sauna tingling and tender, ready for her date with her soldier boyfriend. When she met him, he said, There is no time for rest—a soldier risked his life to sneak out for a bowl of noodles and when he was caught, he shot himself. The soldier asked her to continue waiting.

Of the Millennial Aquarium Built next to the Ocean View Seafood Restaurant

The seafood is so fresh it is alive. The new aquarium is so realistic it looks like a glass tunnel suspended inside the ocean. The parents and child stand on a moving walkway and gawk at a narwhal rapping its tusk against their shoes, a stingray casting a vampiric shadow above their heads, and plankton drifting down around them like celestial matter. Then all is dark and the only source of light is the blind man's eyes of an ancient faced angler fish. Afterward, the parents bring the child to the restaurant and suck out the eggs of dancing shrimp and offer the distressed child a drink from a cold soup of live darting minnows. Everyday, the restaurant offers challenging specials. A man tried to devour a whole writhing octopus as it suctioned around his face and head, his teeth struggling to masticate this all too living body. But he gave up in exhaustion.

Of the Zoo on 6 Chrysanthemum Road

The farmers used to worship the giant pelican which would open its pouched maw to drop down rain. Writers worshipped spotted little men who would whisper fantastic plots in their ears while they slept. We now worship animals that exist. The porcupine. The civet cat. The snake. Even the ant. Our forests are vast empty chambers. Hike to the deepest heart of our mountains and you hear nothing except for the wind's hiss of all that has shamed you. The zoo is the most popular attraction. One zookeeper cares for the only two sea turtles in the world. They are both 100 years old. Everyday, she snaps on gloves and then she gently massages the male turtle so that he may seed one day.

Of the Old Ukrainian Embassy That Will Be Torn Down for the Hanger Factory

Boomtown is Shangdu's brand name. How do you like Boomtown Shangdu? Everyday, 2,000 more people flood into Shangdu to work in our 2,000 factories. Do you know why? Shangdu is booming! Guides will say that twenty years ago, there was nothing but a gas station and a few scattered pig farms along the river. I was one of the few born in Shangdu and it is true what they say about the farms but the guides do not mention how Officials used to dump all the cripples from the Capital into Shangdu. Now that Shangdu is booming, they have rounded all the cripples and exiled them to a remote outpost up north. That outpost is also beginning to boom.

Of the Express Bus Route to the Capital

Yesterday, I almost collided into Rembrandt as the bus sighed its doors open but my mouth was zipped. So I take the same route now, ten minutes earlier, hoping to catch him and sit next to him. But even if I did sit next to him, what would I say? We are not of a culture where curious strangers can strike up a conversation. Love is background checked, set up by services. I tried a service but left once the woman began adding up my worth on a calculator. She still leaves messages on my phone: Why are you so stubborn? There's a waiting list of men here for you. If you return, I'll give you the foreman for half my price.

Of the World's Largest Multilevel Parking Garage

When Officials ignored their strike, the crane operators decided to
be more aggressive. They worked all night. The next morning, train
carriages, buses, limousines, bicycles, boats, and even helicopters swung
lazily in the wind, magnetized by cranes. Negotiate, they cried, and
we will free your vehicles. Finally, Officials promised to bargain but
when meeting day approached, the army rushed into the bargaining
room and all the operators conveniently disappeared. Until Shangdu
finds a new generation of qualified crane operators, no one knows how
to work the cranes and release the vehicles. The magnetized vehicles
sway in the breeze, rust in the rain. One driver was drunkenly passed
out when they lifted his taxi up into the night. He has lost his voice,
calling out to the shuddering city.

Of Future Wireless Highrise 110

For a whole week, I wake to one lone female factory worker protesting
in front of a new construction site next to 88. She shouts into her
bullhorn while sound speakers blast the recording of a cheering crowd.
I flick on a soap on TV and a starlet weeps operatically and drowns
out the recorded crowd. Then I hear the police sirens drowning out
the starlet and the recorded crowd. Cut to the next morning, where the
starlet weeps again on the radio, but it is a rerun, and the construction
site is empty.

Of the Gamblers Den in the Back of 4 Turtle Alley

Once, Officials praised the first enthusiastic student who signed up for the revolution. But then the student said, I noticed that the engineering professor is on your hit list. I will hunt him down and murder him! They cautioned against his choice of the word "murder" and encouraged him to be more inclusive with his targets. As it turned out, the student's wife had run off with the engineering professor. The revolution was quite convenient for the student.

But the professor was wilier than the student and immediately went into hiding with the student's wife. Throughout the year, the student carried a hay cutter and searched obsessively for the professor. His heart twitched in his rib cage as he knocked on every home, showing them a photo of the professor. None of the villagers knew who he was but promised to promptly kill the enemy once they spotted him. No, he begged, If you see him, keep him alive until I return. It wasn't until ten years later that he found him working as a latrine cleaner in Shangdu, which was still a remote outpost. It was said that the professor was so weak that he keeled over before the student nicked him with the cutter. By that time, the revolution was already a month past. The Officials decided that the professor was no longer an enemy and had planned to reinstate him for a government position. They arrested the student and convicted him of murder. As he faced the firing squad, the student realized that he had forgotten to ask what happened to his wife.

Of All the Highrises

Every highrise lacks something. Highrise II has no heat, Highrise 22 lacks floors, Highrise 33 has no spigots, Highrise 44 lacks windowpanes, Highrise 55 lacks stove ranges, while Highrise 66 is lopsided. Highrise 77 is right across from 88 and it is dark as a tomb. It temporarily has no electricity. Sometimes, I see a flicker of candles, roaming flashlights. 77 watches us in the sullen dark, we with our brazenly exposed units. They watch us eat, quarrel, make love, sleep. They watch us watching them. Lately there have been more residents leaping to their deaths out of 88 and spooked 88 residents have been moving to 77, preferring the dark. Some residents of 88 have wrapped a weave of laundry twine in a frail attempt to create a rail. Someone has chosen to wall herself in with stacked urns.

Of the Mega C-City Supermarket

Whenever I am in the grocery store, I see an old man in a wheelchair who weeps in front of an aisle of energy drinks. He is a resident of lopsided Highrise 66, where they have placed all the octogenarians. Old man, I asked one day, why do you weep? The old man choked down his sob. That's me, He said and pointed to the 100 or so energy drinks, each with the same iconic illustration of a young soldier in epaulettes raising his fist. The energy drink is called *Power up!* That's just an illustration, I said. No, he said, those are *my* epaulettes. I was a young soldier during the Campaign and I found and hunted down all the surviving archaeologists. But when the revisionists took over, they sent me to a reeducation camp. I polished those epaulettes with my tears and buried them. And now, they want to remind me of my ways. Why must they remind me so many times?

Of the Central Language Radio Headquarters

Rembrandt only smokes Mild Seven cigarettes. He has a birthmark on his neck, a blue stain intricately shaped like an old-fashioned bicycle where the front wheel is larger than the back. I have imagined this birthmark many times. On a beautiful day in May, when the sun burns through the carbon haze like blood jets from civic posters and white magnolias shoot out like flags from toy guns, we will ride our tall bicycles together.

There is a talk-show hostess who I listen to every night. Every night, people confused by love call to complain and she listens and counsels them with her soothing voice. It used to be women who would seek her advice but lately, it's been men who complain of their unbearable loneliness. Sometimes, they will propose to her and she will laugh gently until they begin to break down.

Rembrandt no longer smokes his Mild Seven cigarettes in front of the factory. The first day I didn't see him, I was mildly worried. Then, a week passed without his presence. My concern became an obsession. Finally, I had the gall to go inside the factory, up to the foreman's office. I pretended I was his cousin and asked for his whereabouts. The foreman sighed with disappointment and said, He was my best painter. But he's gone on to the next city to work at the Renoir factory. He is sick of self-portraits. He wants to paint beautiful women.

Of the Sport Stadium

I sniff my hand and I smell the unfailing scent of Shangdu. How hot
it is, and then how moist, when the rain zithers down and we are all
bonded with our umbrellas. I only work when I don't sleep and now
experience eludes me. Experience eludes me yet somehow, I am full
of shame and I drop my head. Then it happens one after another.
The legions of factory workers and the project managers drop their
heads. The model citizen who announced on TV he will have as many
children as possible to generously spread his genes, drops his head. The
girl dressed as a blue hedgehog in front of the electronic mall drops
her blue hedgehog head. The genetic scientist who claimed to have
cloned the endangered bird drops his head, the crooked moguls drop
their heads and even our transitional leaders drop their heads. A field
of dropped heads. My poppies, my poppies!

The Engineer of Vertical Frontiers

I was born into a donkey, a chicken, then a snotsized
polliwog, born and snorted up a horse's
nostril as it drank from a pond.
Then a foulsome stinker Crusoe washed
onto our shore, crying "Orright!" which Pa,
a lover of all things Brit, christened me:
Orright. I'm Orright.
All noble reckoning pointed to a white-
beamed path: a CEO pa (deemed a fearsome
foe reeducated to his grave),
a swanly ma (a roader's wife, too vain
they cried and drowned her in her own toilettes)
who tenderly scraped my ears of wax with
a tiny spoon stippled with my surname.
Now, I'm not deserving a name.
I'm a titbit, a dollop easily bored,
a trolloping doer, I loll and gag,
fired from the tear gas factory, the denture factory,
now the heart-ticker factory.
I'm not fond of people,
though I'm quite fond of the idea of people.
Inside my bunker, a snow globe in every room.
Inside each globe, a cloudcapt city of silksack
buildings powered by a field of weedsized
turbines so air will be purer than virgins.
Dumb ideas, Pa's cadaver wheezes.
Go back to the factory of dentures, Orright.
Work hard, Orright, work hard.

A Little Tête-à-tête

Coleridge, it is me, your affectionate friend!
Might I interrupt you from your compositions, for a little tête-à-tête,
lure you even, to a tee-off on our emerald
swath of watered, manicured sward?

We have shattered new frontiers with our 14 golf courses.
A dexterous harmony of manmade and natural hazards,
fairway glades surrounded by leafwhelmed mountains
of tinted tallow trees and pars graced with stately flame
throated birds-of-paradise.

And vigilantly raked sand bunkers, so many in one par,
this sand-cratered par looks hauntingly extraterrestrial.
We have a 150 yard beach bunker—sand imported from
the sucrose beaches of the Caribbean!

There are manmade lakes, the water dyed a cool, hushed slate,
pocked with waterfowls and verdant hassocks of island green and a putting
green mown to velvet uniformity.

This will be the world's premier tournament venue,
already visited by Nick Faldo (I have seen a wax likeness of him
at your homeland's Madame Tussaud's), Annika Sorenstam,
and of course, the Great Tiger Woods.

You may notice an absence of golf carts,
but we are currently waiting for the newest generation
of multiple-passenger rough-terrain utility vehicles,
which should arrive next month.

Our temporary solution to this lack is an entrusted,
well-trained army of caddies.
That there, the compact little man in the plaid shorts is Xiao.
Oh, he's not scowling at you, he's scowling at me but he doesn't know
that I know this: *Pig! Better not stir shit up! I'm watching you!*
You must excuse caddies for of course,
they are prone to human error.

Dash off? Why must you dash off?
To dash down what you just dreamed? But my friend,
I've already dreamed up this Xanadu,
a mere 40 miles from Shangdu, with the profits of my lint rollers
and rolls of polysynthetic fur! Oh, I see: every second
you stall until you write your opiate dream down,
your Elysian visions will escape your grasp,
and your verse will finish leadenly.

Allow me to wipe the crusted sleep from your eyes with my thumbs.
When I was a child, I had untreated pinkeye and my ma
used to wipe the mucus tearing from my eyes, while she smoked her
endless cigarettes to calm the parasites in her stomach.
Outside Shangdu, we have a sprawl
of Country Housing Garden estates. My little girl lives
in one of these houses, wishing to be a poet like you.
Will you go and tutor her? I will pay you handsomely.
I always tell her, you must practice everyday.
She practices, everyday.

Gift

Sister, you will not approve but my lover
is the last surviving, mannerly hearted archaeologist.

It began when he kindly gave me a tour
of his home and unrolled a ball of gold-crushed sash to shew
me the rarest-of-all artifact:

a narwal's horn, carved with a battle scene of 400 men on horseback.
The relief's details so delicately whorled and fretted,
I could detect the scale on every blood-stained armor,
the teeth on each neighing, reeling horse
and even the vessels in a driven warrior's eyes.

He said Once Shangdu was a city of craftsmanship,
They bartered carvings and ink whose properties were proven
to be fatal, he said, when scholars were punished
and forced to drink them straight.
*

Together, we wander the open-air market.
They hawk outdated tracts as nostalgic curios:
The People's Creed, The People's Deeds, The People's Needs.

Other than tracts and electronic gadgets—DVD players
in every variation and also, DVDs of every genre—
apothecaries have set up shop, hocking ointments
like teatree oil to ward off mosquitoes,
ointments claimed to be made of seal blubber
to cure inflamed thyroids, balms as natural birth control,
and imported cold medicines tha'taste
like wincing sweet cherries.

All quackery, the archaeologist warned me, except for the scents,
and bought me a vintage seagreen atomizer bottle with a knitted squeeze bulb.
We were the first to import tea roses, he said,
and before I spritzed the rich perfume

he said, When I die, I want you to wear tha' smell
since it will explode with the memories
of our time together.

I blushed at his sentimentality.
*

I should think it a favor if you not tell Ma of my affair—
I will come to a decision with marriage soon enough.

Of course, the archaeologist is much too old for me.
Really, I have many suitors here including
a Christian which you might think queer,

but these are odd times, Sister.
People are beginning to believe in gods and godheads
churches with fattened coffers have been shut down and have
swiftly reopened as profitable enterprises.

The Christian who pangs for me hands out tracts to passersby,
a tract of a different kind. He is also a craftsman,
carving the most intricate miniature men
and gifting them to me.

Seed Seller's Sonnet

My mind slides like a sword in my mouth
and I awake caked in spit.
Shangdu's choked with blokes, not enough dames.
I am generations old yet—
                 I am a virgin.
Tripey thoughts wrack my loins.
I am a runt squeaming for a grim little teat.

Though once I was so decent from such humble backgrounds,
my ma bit her arm to feed us brothers three.
Am I cursed? I drink the myrrh   her life   who forced me alive.
History intones catch up, catch up   while a number rots, then another.

Beautiful bicycles, city of broken spokes, a thousand women floated to heaven.
Then I had a most marvelous piece of luck   I died.

THE
WORLD
CLOUD

Come Together

Snow like pale cephalopods drifts down
as it melts into our lapels we are all connected
into a shared dream where we
don't need our heirloom
mouths.

In imagining the future,
we once desired a ziggurat to crumble
into the oil spoilt sea while a muscled Austrian
demanded that we get inside the last
working chopper.

But everywhere around us, immaculate
snow dusts the blue pine trees, industry
is now invisible behind a wall
of woven passwords

and outside the blue-tiled courtyard,
a mother rubs her child's eyelids with lotion
and the lonely child dreams of having one friend
to share cherry ice cones
in winter

then she dreams about suicide and who will
be the saddest who will cry the hardest
it is a death that she rehearses
many times but there
is no time to reflect,

only react so lick my hot cortex, love,
now my imagination can be any nation I want,
though I try so hard to prove myself,
I pull a muscle.

Hear hovercrafts fizz along glass tunnels
rockets zip through skies like darning needles
do we possibly have such endless fuel,
why look at these pelicans.

Still, chimes the Prophet, that spill
won't slow the whale of progress!
Water will clean itself and human
consciousness will shift
imperceptibly.

There go the people, said the bookkeeper
I must follow them for I am the leader
and into the horizon
he'll go swallowed.

Year of the Amateur

Recall the frontier inside us when the business
of memory booms, when broadbands uncoil
and clouds swell with sticky portals, amassing
to a monsoon of live-streams.
Burn your chattel to keep the cloud afloat
so its tears can freeze to snow.
The voice flatlines in this season of pulp:
The artist makes miniature churches out of drain pulp,
the Indonesian rainforest is pulped,
the last illuminated gold leaves are pulped so we
gather and watch an otter nibble
sweet urchin to a pulp.
We laugh softly.

Engines Within the Throne

We once worked as clerks
       scanning moth-balled pages
into the clouds, all memories
outsourced except the fuzzy
       childhood bits when

I was an undersized girl with a tic,
they numbed me with botox
       I was a skinsuit
of dumb expression, just fingerprints
over my shamed

       all I wanted was snow
to snuff the sun blades to shadow spokes,
muffle the drum of freeways, erase
       the old realism

but this smart snow erases
       nothing, seeps everywhere,
the search engine is inside us,
the world is our display

       and now every industry
has dumped whole cubicles, desktops,
fax machines into developing
       worlds where they stack
them as walls against

what disputed territory
        we asked the old spy who drank
with Russians to gather information
the old-fashioned way,

now we have snow sensors,
        so you can go spelunking
in anyone's mind,
let me borrow your child

thoughts, it's benign surveillance,
        I can burrow inside, find a cave
pool with rock-colored flounder,
and find you, half-transparent
with depression.

A Visitation

You are at home.
You are wearing bicycle shorts though you don't own a bike.
Outside your window, you see a flower you don't recognize.
The voice of Gregory Peck booms: Honey Suckle.
You don't know anything anymore.
You remember an old trivia show you watched when you were young.
The contestant went to Stanford.
You remember his name: Stan Chan.
The first question was always absurdly easy,
almost as if it was testing your listening skills.
The host asked Stan Chan what a nectarine
was closest to: a. orange, b. peach, c. banana, d. grape.
Stan chuckled: Well, I think I should know this one. It's a. orange.
You remember the host's expression.
You look at the toaster and think taco.
An ad pops up in the air for a trip to Cabo San Lucas.
The snow is still beta.
You feel the smart snow monitoring you,
uploading your mind so anyone can access your content.
Circuits cross and you hear a one-sided chat:
Da! Da! Da!
You tap in the air for the volume control and listen to Ravel.
You refresh your feed. Nothing from him.
It is too hot here.
You hate this satellite Californian town
near the satellite tech campus where you and your husband
used to work as data scanners.
When they laid both of you off,
you tried work as freelancers from your home offices.
You used to chirp at each other like demented birds.
Another chime.

It's a real chime.
A man delivering your groceries: a dozen cantaloupes.
He looks like your husband.
You think of inviting him in.
Why did you order a dozen cantaloupes?
You hear a woman crying.
Lately, you've been fascinated by a user-generated hologram:
an ethnically ambiguous boy who pretends to drop dead from a shoot-out.
The boy wakes up when his mother comes home.
She scolds him and turns off the camera.
You blink to go offline.
It is like all the quiet Sundays of your childhood.
You think you hear your husband sigh but he's only breathing.
He used to stare into the middle distance
for weeks until you lugged him to bed.
You tucked him in.

The Infinite Reply

I speak in shorthand
       clips of sequels
branding voice to acronym
       on long-horn steer roaming the open
source of our collective creation
what domain do you live in
little post-it

In a landscape of reminders
reminding the novelist to say
       I write in direct osmosis
from writer to reader no bric-a-brac
       wall of words blown
by tech giants who say choice

       is a tool like a blade of grass
poked in a log hole for protein-rich bugs
       flicking to irritation
when nothing will load
so out you go to stinging sunshine
       finding relief in the cereal aisle
filling your mind with boarders
       who rush in when
breakfast bells chime.

Ready-Made

I tint the street view a forgiving dove
        since nothing fades to twilit
oblivion, so zoom in until my eyes
        need moisturizing

the sitting room is quiet, sprayed
with air freshener the flavor of aged
        card catalogue,
glass shelves full of tooled tell-alls
have transcended

        into the data air
sealed into capsules you can skim
while eating a nuked pot pie,
        even alone, you're self-conscious
of eating alone, so you

try to look busy, dialing the help desk
        chatting with a timed
Indian accent until the line
        goes dead, though

nothing ever goes dead,
        smart snow has reached
total density, drifting even inside
the hospice so you hear

the gray-eyed pulse
of comas, private as a cargo of stones
        being dragged across the arctic,
the orphaned, fugitive voice
whispering *enough, leave me*

in a company retreat,
cuffed in the legs, partners bumbling
toward a finishing line, teamwork
so harmonious

the booming trade of information
exists without our paid labor
what to do with all this leisure
I blink at my orange trees

spangled with captions,
landscapes overlaid
with golden apps and speculation
nudging hope like the sham

time machinist who returns from
the future, convincing
everyone with his doctored
snapshots of restored

prosperity and a sea full
of whales huge as ocean liners
singing the call-note of our
relieved tears.

Who's Who

You wake up from a nap.
Your mouth feels like a cheap acrylic sweater.
You blink online and 3-D images hopscotch around you.
A telenovela actress hides under your lampshade.
You switch to voice activation.
Good Afternoon! Sings the voice of Gregory Peck.
You look out your window, across the street.
Faded mattresses sag against a chain-link fence.
The mattress seller sits on a crate, clipping his fingernails.
You think of inviting him in.
You do a scan.
Gregory Peck booms: Dwayne Healey, 28, convicted felon of petty larceny.
You don't know what to do so you pet your ceramic cat.
What? You ask. What? You want to go out? Well you can't.
You hear a chime.
It is your former employer informing you that they cannot release
your husband's password due to the Privacy Policy.
It is their 98th auto reply.
You bite your hand.
You check in on your husband.
After your husband went on roam, you received one message from him:
I am by a pond and a coyote is eating a frog. It's amazing.
You decide to go outside.
You walk to the public park.
There is a track where people run while watching whatever
they're watching.
You sit on an oversized bench.
You think of your old town house with the oatmeal sofa
before you and husband downgraded to this neighborhood.
The sofa made you happy.
You decide you need to keep up appearances.

You need to clip your husband's nails. They are getting long.
A strangled *yip* escapes from you and a jogger stares at you.
You see a palm tree and it is carved up with little penis drawings.
You make a sound like tut-tut.
You enhance the park.
You fill in the balding grass and rub the offensive drawings
from the tree. You add coconuts.
You feel your insides are being squeezed out through a tiny hole
the size of a mosquito bite.
You hear children laughing as they rush out of a bus and it sounds
far away and watery, like how it used to in the movies, when the light was haloey,
and it was slow-motion, and the actor was having a terrible flashback.
But you are not having a flashback.
Underneath the sound of children laughing, you hear users chatting
over each other, which all blurs into a warring shadow of insects
and the one that sounds like a hornet is your husband,
telling you to put his stuff in storage.
Or sell it to pay off bills or
leave, why don't you goddamn leave.
You sit on the bench until the sky turns pink.
When your former employer let you go,
they said, you are now free to pursue what you want to pursue.
So here you are.

A Wreath of Hummingbirds

I suffer a different kind of loneliness.
From the antique ringtones of singing
wrens, babbling babies, and ballad medleys,
my ears have turned
to brass.

They resurrect a thousand extinct birds:
emus, dodos, and shelducks, though some,
like the cerulean glaucous macaw,
could not survive the snow. How heavily
they roost on trees in raw twilight.

I will not admire those birds,
not when my dull head throbs, and I am plagued
by sorrow, a green hummingbird eats me alive
with its stinging needle beak.

Then I meet you. Our courtship is fierce
and indiscreet in a prudish city that scorns our love,
as if the ancient laws of miscegenation
are still in place. I am afraid
I will infect you

after a virus clogs the gift economy:
booming etrade of flintlock guns sag.
Status updates flip from we are all
connected to we are exiles.
What bullshit

when in that same prudish city,
they have one exact word to describe the shades
of their sorrow, when they always sit together
and eat cold noodles during white
days of rain, always in one long table,
though not all

as a boy, my father used to trap
little brown sparrows, bury them in hot coal,
and slowly eat the charred birds alone
in the green fields, no sounds,
no brothers in sight.

Holiest are those who eat alone.
Do not hurt them, do not push them, insult them,
do not even stare at them, leave
them to eat alone, in peace.

The Golden State

Here you are deep
inside the marrow of song
      a spirit shape tucked
in my ear before snow

streams an old-time town
      a general store selling cornmeal
      and used dentures
what time zone is this

home of sad marvels,
      pluck my memory out,
I am just immigrant enough
      to feel shame

for my overseas kin who live inside gaming
and still their warriors are listless,
      brooding
you cannot speak

      her brimmed mind
she went hysterically blind
      so they implanted an ocularis
and she said I see light
sharpening

to contours, a field,
marigolds, golden poppies,
      I see their names
but why do I smell smoke

in the engine, the way memory
        will just hit
I unvalve the escape hatch
          a gentle hiss

breathing in a remote dark
          planet, suck in,
come back.

The Quattrocento

I hail an aerocab,
turn up my personalized surround sound
track: wistful to anthemic
to voice
          recognition,
a song strains after a longed
sweet spot of identification.
          O parable diced three ways
          I want to share my thoughts
with you and formal
          you so wander outward
          into the mesquite frontier preserved
in sprawl
          out on my cub rug, my domain,
          the room thrums with zither
the thip of pick against rack of strings
          a sample free to share
including versions
          of California would you like
an aerial footage of clouds
          the mild color of jicama see
your face in their formations
          before focus

          is a new commodity
the focus groups agree my attention lasts
as long as parents are concerned
          that all towns now are rest stops
          to a vanishing point
we're all going to the clouds,
          haunted by a gobbet

of flesh marooned
on the glass surface of image
　　　you can now feel the hologram
like skinned grapes in a haunted
　　　town where industry
was once material

fallout is invisible snow, *nieve*,
　　　der schnee, noon, pricked
by silver neuronic snow,
　　　I am accentless
　　　chat with me the voice
activation is on so too the translation
conversion of euro
　　　to the falling currency
of American fragments
I don't want to be a niche
　　　I want to be a yardstick
become the voice

　of the carefree surfer riding the winter waves
　　　in his gimp suit.
There is no moon, unless I dim you out
　　　like a dimmer you prat what part of
my password is weak
　　　like your abs, you
half-eaten child living
　　　in a torso of live-cams
you think your head is legendary
everyone can see you

　　　see the brightest tree
of you, you everywhere
　　　your face I interface

massage into being, sprouting mouth
after raw mouth, lidless
nervous system, sunlit band
      width of ancestors surveying
      the bright, unbound
presence of the new world,
      trampling thrush
my heart fills with water
      swallowing it
whole.

Get Away from It All

Go, go, I breathe the air
        flossed with silence
moving me to melt

into any form what
        choice when they
finish your thought

did you mean numerous no
        numinous
when minds flood into minds
yet one creed molds

this town of giant convenience
        a white church
of blond wooden pews burning

a dark pile of something
        enough these terrors,
clarity, empathy, please

drop me onto a quiet coast
        dotted with sandpipers
the horizon hyphenates

are they UN forces no
        they are nudist bathers.
They have beached.
Dashed with amorous wet,

they call out like walruses,
these loafing rebels against
            the enhanced,
I see too much

yet go, go into the unknown,
            smell the salt, rancid
scent of water, seagull,
blades of grass and listen,

the one with the sodden beard says
            undrape yourself,
you are not guilty to me.

✿   ✿   ✿

Fable of the Last Untouched Town

I.

We are the only hole in a world of light.
No lamps grid our streets, no cars flash their headlights.
When sun sets, we have no choice
but to resign ourselves.

There are those who dread the night, who grow mad
with boredom during the long winter months
when the shrieking wind and dark cut
the wilted day at noon.

I prefer night. We are more invisible then.
He and I take our strolls at night,
traveling far out to the abandoned spas where old tourists
used to come and ablute themselves
to relieve their bones.

We speculate what has happened to them.
We heard wild rumors.
People live to 150. They grow hearts
out of cells.

All those hours we talk.
Sitting in the wide, cracked basins that used to hold
the prized green water,
(it was nothing but dyed faucet water)
now littered with the slimy leaves of gingko.

2.

In this town, we are impervious to discomfort

such as the cold that crackles our blanket
and beards the loudspeakers with ice, freezing
the monthly bloody rags women dry for the night.

We are strong, not afraid to betray.
For instance, we rush our old.

I wrap my mother in blankets:
It's time now Mother.
I'm not ready.
Oh but your mind is going, your tongue
is loosening you will start to talk we planned this.
I'm not ready to go.

My brother carries her up the mountain of junipers.
I make a nest for her.
I dread that we will see other kin abandoned there
I already see her tongue
dotted with frostbite yet we leave her
as she calls and calls.

As we trudge back down, our breaths wild
we chant songs of our king.

3.

Then the man who I used to go for walks with
also disappeared.
I suppose I loved him or once, once
I did.

Mothers, fathers, friends, lovers.
No fairy stories to ease children's ears.
We are to say: Enemies of the state.
No sorrows and songs, no

he's gone far away to somewhere magical.
Our people are dancing a ring around a tower
and he is the tower. He is the tree.

I have dreams. A blade cold
as ice-nettled milk steaming inside a neck.
I am afraid that they could read my dreams.

I volunteer to collect night soil.

Mountains of frozen shit.
I shovel them into buckets and spread them
over the yellow fields and out of waste,
comes food for the only God
we know.

4.

A storm raged for a week and our town was erased
by hills of snow.
Afar, our one story chambered apartments
look like concrete harmonicas. It's easy for snow to swallow us.

But after the storm, a gigantic glacier appeared inside
the king's most cherished open-air stadium.
It took up the whole arena.

Our leader launched a campaign.
Defunct factories suddenly produced heat lamps
and they strung a ceiling of scalding tubed bulbs over the stadium,
but the glacier only glistened.

So he demanded legions of laborers to come
chip away at this offensive glacier.
I was drafted to help.

When I arrived, I was awed, I was so awed, I began to cry
but when someone questioned my tears,
I said I was crying for our king and cursed
the imperialist-plotted ice.

The sheer sapphire cliffstone towered so high,
the whole ocean seemed frozen inside it.
Under its shellacked panes of ice were marblings of color
I'd long forgotten: tangerine, topaz,
canary and rose.

Like fluorescing cuttlefish,
the colors pulsed, swirled and bloomed
into contracting rings. The ice breathed.

We slowly chipped away with our picks.
As soon as we gathered a pile,
the wind burst in and scattered the powdery snow far
into the air like spores.

One laborer accidentally swallowed ice
and it caused him to hallucinate, blither in another language.
He was immediately exterminated.
We were forced to wear masks.

One day, I decided to steal some.
I pocketed one grain.

The snow glowed bluely in my hovel.
My little lamp.
Then one night I don't know why I swallowed it.

And this is what I saw.

Notes

"Of the Millennial Promenade Along the River": Image inspired by Walid Raad's "I Only Wish I Could Weep."

"Of the Millennial Aquarium Built next to the Ocean View Seafood Restaurant": Image inspired by Park Chan-wook's *Old Boy*.

"A Little Tête-à-tête": A response to Samuel Taylor Coleridge's "Kubla Khan."

"The Quattrocento": In Korean, *noon* translates to both "snow" and "eye."